CRASH BANDICOOT:

HERO OF WUMPA ISLAND

x1996

Kenny Abdo

Fly!
An Imprint of Abdo Zoom
abdobooks.com

abdobooks.com

Published by Abdo Zoom, a division of ABDO, P.O. Box 398166, Minneapolis, Minnesota 55439. Copyright © 2022 by Abdo Consulting Group, Inc. International copyrights reserved in all countries. No part of this book may be reproduced in any form without written permission from the publisher. Fly!™ is a trademark and logo of Abdo Zoom.

Printed in the United States of America, North Mankato, Minnesota.
102021
012022

THIS BOOK CONTAINS RECYCLED MATERIALS

Photo Credits: Alamy, Everett Collection, Getty Images, iStock, KrimaDraws, newscom, Shutterstock, Wikimedia
Production Contributors: Kenny Abdo, Jennie Forsberg, Grace Hansen
Design Contributors: Candice Keimig, Neil Klinepier

Library of Congress Control Number: 2021940188

Publisher's Cataloging-in-Publication Data

Names: Abdo, Kenny, author.
Title: Crash Bandicoot: hero of Wumpa Island / by Kenny Abdo
Other Title: hero of Wumpa Island
Description: Minneapolis, Minnesota : Abdo Zoom, 2022 | Series: Video game heroes | Includes online resources and index.
Identifiers: ISBN 9781098226923 (lib. bdg.) | ISBN 9781644947371 (pbk.) | ISBN 9781098227760 (ebook) | ISBN 9781098228187 (Read-to-Me ebook)
Subjects: LCSH: Video game characters--Juvenile literature. | Crash Bandicoot (Game)-Juvenile literature. | Sony Playstation video games--Juvenile literature. | Heroes-Juvenile literature.
Classification: DDC 794.8--dc23

TABLE OF CONTENTS

CRASH BANDICOOT

Crushing boxes and scarfing down **Wumpa** fruit, there is no video game hero like Crash Bandicoot.

As the official mascot of the first PlayStation, Crash has been entertaining gamers for many decades!

PLAYER PROFILE

Jason Rubin

Creators Andy Gavin and Jason Rubin wanted to make a game that was fun and cartoon-like. Inspiration was taken from Tasmanian Devil from *Looney Tunes* and Sonic the Hedgehog.

Gavin and Rubin first created Willie the Wombat. But the character grew and changed into a bandicoot during production.

Crash became the symbol of Sony's PlayStation. However, CEO Ken Kutaragi never wanted the company to have a mascot. Especially not Crash Bandicoot. But he had no idea how important the character would be for decades to come.

LEVEL
UP

Crash Bandicoot was released in 1996. Unlike Kutaragi, fans went crazy for the orange hero! The game sold more than six-million copies worldwide. It is one of the best-selling PlayStation games of all time!

Crash Bandicoot: Cortex Strikes Back was in the works before the first game was even released. It was also a massive hit. A third game, *Warped*, quickly followed.

NEW GAME
LOAD GAME

The **franchise** dipped into racing and party **platforms**. First to come was *Crash Team Racing* in 1999. It was followed by *Crash Bash* in 2000.

For the next 15 years, Crash would star in 13 other games. They included **remasters** of his classics. In 2008, he would take a break from new adventures.

Crash came back in 2020 with *Crash Bandicoot 4: It's About Time*. Fans were ready to have him back! In 2021, Crash went mobile with *On the Run!*

EXPANSION PACK

Crash Bandicoot was the first **third-person** game where the player was behind the character. It paved the way for games like *Last of Us* and *Gears of War*.

Crash became the mascot for the
Leukemia & Lymphoma Society in
2007. He is used to raise awareness
of the diseases among young people.

In 2012, a 15-million-year-old bandicoot fossil was uncovered in Australia. The team gave the species the name *Crash bandicoot*, proving the orange hero has influence off-screen too!

GLOSSARY

CEO – short for Chief Executive Officer. A person in charge of managing a company.

fossil – the preserved remains of something that lived or existed a long time ago.

franchise – a collection of related video games in a series.

Leukemia & Lymphoma Society – a charitable organization that is dedicated to fighting blood cancer and improving the lives of patients.

platform – a type or style of video game.

remaster – a video game franchise that has been updated with newer technology.

species – living things that are very much alike.

third-person – when the view is outside of the character's body.

Wumpa – a fictional fruit created for the Crash games. It is a combination of apples and mangos.

ONLINE RESOURCES

Booklinks
NONFICTION NETWORK
FREE! ONLINE NONFICTION RESOURCES

To learn more about Crash Bandicoot, please visit abdobooklinks.com or scan this QR code. These links are routinely monitored and updated to provide the most current information available.

INDEX